Pa:
Gastronomique:
Spain/Portugal

G. Tavares, P. Torres, J. Albertson

5th Edition

For comments, suggestions or corrections please write to:
info@travelightbooks.com

Travelight Books

Dining in Spain

Reserving a Table

I (we) have a reservation. *Tengo (tenemos) una reserva.*

Do you have a table for one (two)? *¿Tiene una mesa para uno (dos)?*

I'd like a quiet table. *Me gustaría una mesa tranquila.*

I would like a table for ___, please. *Una mesa para ___, por favor.*

I would like to reserve a table for___ *Quisiera reservar una mesa para ___*

-**one** *una persona*

-**two** *dos personas*

-**three** *tres personas*

-**four** *cuatro personas*

-**five** *cinco personas*

-**six** *seis personas*

Doneness of Meat

Well done *bien hecho*

Rare *poco hecho*

Medium *medio hecho*

Medium rare *poco a medio cocido*

Utensils

Spoon *cuchara*

Fork *tenedor*

Knife *cuchillo*

Drinking glass *vaso/copa*

Cup *taza*

Plate *plato*

Bowl *tazón/escudilla*
Napkin *servilleta*

Meals

Breakfast *desayuno*
Lunch *comida*
Dinner *cena*
Snack *bocado*
Menu of the day, with fixed courses & price *Menú del día*
Fixed-price meal *comida fija-preciada*
À la carte (items ordered separately) *a la carta*

Special Dining Requests

I am a vegetarian *Yo soy vegetariano/a (m/f)*
I do not eat meat *Yo no como carne*
I am gluten-intolerant. Do you have any dishes that include no wheat, barley or rye? *Tengo una intolerancia al gluten. ¿Tiene algunos platos que no incluyen trigo, cebada o centeno?*
Do you have any dishes suitable for a vegetarian (vegan)? *¿Tiene algunos platos aptos para un vegetariano (vegan)?*
I do not eat............ *Yo no como ....*
I am allergic to.......... *Soy alérgico a ....*
I cannot eat any food containing............ *No puedo comer cualquier alimento que contenga ....*
  -shellfish *mariscos*
  -milk products *productos lácteos*
  -gluten *gluten*
  -raw fish *pescado crudo*

-raw meat *carne cruda*

-eggs huevos

-meat *carne*

-sesame seeds *semillas de sésamo*

-soy *soja*

-peanuts *cacahuetes*

-nuts *nueces*

-fish *pescado*

-strawberries *fresas*

-tomatoes *tomates*

-wheat *trigo*

-beef *carne de vacuno*

-corn (maize) *maíz*

May I see the menu, please? *¿Puedo ver el menú, por favor?*

Is there a specialty of this restaurant? *¿Hay alguna especialidad de la casa?*

Is there a regional specialty? *¿Hay alguna especialidad regional?*

What is the soup of the day? *¿Cuál es la sopa del día?*

What do you recommend? *¿Qué me recomienda?*

I want _____. *Quiero _____.*

I wish to have a dish with _____. *Quisiera un plato que lleve _____.*

-Noodles *fideos*

-Rice *arroz*

-Beans *frijoles, habichuelas*

-Vegetables *verdura*

-Pork *Cerdo*

-Lamb *cordero*

-Chicken *pollo*

-**Beef** *ternera, vacuno, res*

-**Fish** *pescado*

-**Ham** *jamón (J pronounced as H)*

-**Sausage** *salchicha*

-**Cheese** *queso*

-**Eggs** *huevos*

May I have a bottle of __? *¿Me puede poner una botella de __?*

-**Juice** *zumo (Z is pronounced TH)*

-**Water** *agua*

-**Sparkling water** *agua con gas*

-**Agua mineral** *bottled mineral water*

-**Beer** *cerveza*

-**Red/white wine** *vino tinto/blanco*

-**Milk** *la leche*

May I have a glass of ____? *¿Me puede poner un vaso de ____?*

-**Milk** *la leche*

-**Juice** *zumo (Z is pronounced TH)*

-**Water** *agua*

-**Sparkling water** *agua con gas*

-**Agua mineral** *bottled mineral water*

-**Beer** *cerveza*

-**Red/white wine** *vino tinto/blanco*

May I have a cup of ____? *¿Me puede poner una taza de ____?*

-**Coffee** *café*

-**Tea (drink)** *té*

May I have some ____? *¿Me puede dar un poco de ____?*

-**Butter** *mantequilla*

-**Salt** *sal*

-**Pepper** *pimienta*

-**Salad** *ensalada*

I ordered this rare (medium-rare, medium, well-done) *Pedí este poco hecho (poco a medio cocido, medio cocido, bien hecho)*

This is undercooked. *Esto es casi crudo*

This is overcooked. *Esto es cocido demasiado*

I don't think we ordered this *No creo que hemos pedido esto*

I think there's a mistake on the bill *Creo que hay un error en la factura*

Waiter! *¡Camarero!*

Waitress! *¡Camarera!*

Paying the Tab

Waiter! *¡camarero!*

I'm finished. *terminé*

It was delicious. *Muy bueno* or *Estuvo delicioso*

May I have the check, please. *La cuenta, por favor.*

Where are the washrooms? *¿Dónde están los servicios?*

Where is the toilet? *¿Dónde están los aseos?*

Ordering Drinks

May we have some tap water (mineral water) *¿Nos puedes traer un poco de agua de grifo (agua mineral)*

May I have a beer, please. *Una cerveza, por favor.*

Two beers, please. *Dos cervezas, por favor.*

A glass of red wine. *Un vaso de vino tinto.*

A glass of white wine. *Un vaso de vino blanco.*

Two glasses of red/white wine. *Dos vasos de vino tinto/ blanco.*

A bottle. *Una botella.*

Water *agua*
Tonic water *agua tónica*
Orange juice *jugo de naranja (J pronounced H)*
Coke *Coca-Cola*
Refresco *Soda*
Beer *Cerveza*
Cuba Libre *Rum and Coke*
Cubata *Whiskey and Coke*
Whiskey *Whisky*
Vodka *Vodka*
Rum *Ron*
Another drink, please. *Otro, por favor.*
Another round, please. *Otra ronda, por favor.*
Where is the toilet? *¿Dónde están los aseos?*

Useful Words & Phrases

Please *Por favor*

Thank you *Gracias*

You're welcome *De nada*

Yes *Sí*

No *No*

Hello *Hola (H is silent)*

Good morning *Buenos días*

Good afternoon or **Good evening** *Buenas tardes*

Good evening or **Good night** *Buenas noches*

Have a good day *Que pase un buen día*

How are you? *¿Cómo está?*

I'm fine, thank you *Muy bien, gracias.*

What is your name? *¿Cómo se llama usted? (LL sounds like Y)*

My name is _____ *Me llamo* _____

Nice to meet you *Encantado/a (m/f)*

It's a pleasure to meet you *Mucho gusto*

Excuse me *Disculpe*

I beg your pardon *Perdone*

May I get by? *Permiso*

I'm sorry *Lo siento*

Goodbye *Adiós* or *hasta luego*

Do you speak English? *¿Hablas inglés?*

I don't understand *No entiendo*

Where is the toilet? *¿Dónde están los aseos?*

Tapas

Aceitunas *Mixed olives*

Aceitunas a la Madrileña *Olives Madrid style, usu. black, pitted in oil and vinegar with garlic, paprika and oregano*

Albondigas *Meatballs, often in a tomato sauce*

Allioli *Means "garlic and oil" in Catalan. The classic ingredients are only garlic, oil and salt, but the common form of it includes Mayonnaise and garlic. A very strong garlic paste. Served on bread or with potatoes, fish, meat or grilled vegetables.*

Almejas a la Murciana *Murcian style clams, small clams in a sauce of white wine, garlic, red pepper flakes and onion*

Almejas a la Pescadora *Clams fisherman-style, clams in a thickened sauce of white wine, lemon, nutmeg, garlic, red pepper flakes and onion*

Anchoas *anchovies*

Bacalao con Pueros Caramelizados y Naranja *Cod with caramelized leek and orange*

Bacalao *Salted cod loin sliced very thinly, usually served with bread and tomatoes*

Banderillas *A Spanish tapa, small skewers with various ingredients, may include olives, small onions, anchovies, tuna, etc.*

Berenjena con Pollo y Pimientos *Eggplant with chicken and peppers*

Berenjena con Vinagreta de Tomate *Grilled eggplant in tomato vinaigrette*

Boquerones *White anchovies served in vinegar (boquerones en vinagre) or deep fried.*

Calamares Fritos or Calamares a la Romana *Fried squid*

Calamares or rabas *Rings of battered squid*

Cangrejos de Rio con Tomate *Crayfish in tomato sauce*

Carne mechada *Slow-cooked, tender beef*

Chopitos *Battered and fried tiny squid. Also known as puntillitas.*

Chorizo a la sidra *Chorizo sausage slowly cooked in cider.*

Chorizo al vino *Chorizo sausage slowly cooked in wine.*

Chorizo *Spanish red spicy pork sausage, of different varieties. Can be hot (in red wine sauce) or cold.*

Cojonuda *A kind of "pincho". It consists of a slice of Spanish morcilla with a fried quail egg over a slice of bread. It is very common in Burgos, because the most well known and widespread Spanish morcilla is from there. In can also be prepared with a little strip of red spicy pepper.*

Cojonudos *Fried quail eggs with chorizo or morcilla*

Cojonudo *A kind of "pincho". It consists of a slice of Spanish chorizo with a fried quail egg over a slice of bread.*

Cojonudos y Cojonudas *Fried quail eggs with chorizo or morcilla*

Croquetas *Croquettes are a common sight on bar counters across Spain, served as a tapa, light lunch, or a dinner along with a salad.*

Croquetas de Jamón *Ham croquettes*

Empanadas Gallegas *Tuna or meat filled turnover pastry*

Empanadas or empanadillas *large or small turnovers filled with meats and vegetables.*

Ensaladilla Rusa *Russian Salad: made with mixed boiled vegetables with tuna, olives and mayonnaise.*

Gambas al Ajillo *Shrimp in garlic*

Gambas *Shrimps sautéed in salsa negra (peppercorn sauce), al*

ajillo (with garlic), or
pil-pil (with chopped chili
peppers).

**Hojaldre Relleno de
Marisco** *Seafood-filled
pastry*

**Huevos Rellenos de
Gambas** *Deviled eggs
with shrimp*

**Jamon, Queso y Chorizo
con Pan** *Ham, cheese
and chorizo with bread*

Jamon *Spanish ham of
different varieties, usually
cured.*

Langostinos Cocidos
Boiled prawns

Magro *Pieces of pork in
tomato sauce.*

**Mejillones en Vinagreta
de Tomate** *Mussels in
tomato vinaigrette*

Mejillones Rellenos
"Tigres" - stuffed mussels

**Papas Arrugadas / Papas
con Mojo** *New potatoes
boiled in salt water, then
drained, slightly roasted
and served with Mojo
sauce, a garlic, paprika,
red pepper, cumin seed,
olive oil, wine vinegar,
salt and bread crumbs*

(without the crust) to
thicken it.

Patatas Alioli *Alioli
potatoes*

Patatas bravas *Crispy
potato cubes served with
a spicy tomato sauce,
often served with aioli.*

**Pimientos de
Padrón** *Small green
peppers from Padrón (a
town in the province of
Coruña) that are fried in
olive oil. Most are very
mild, but a few in each
batch are quite spicy.*

**Pimientos Rellenos de
Atun** *Red peppers stuffed
with tuna*

**Pimientos Rojos con
Anchoas** *Red peppers
with anchovies*

Pincho moruno *A spicy
kebab-like stick, made of
pork or chicken. Its name
means 'Moorish Stick'.*

**Potaje de Garbanzos y
Espinacas** *Garbanzo
and spinach soup*

Pulpa *octopus tentacle
rings*

Pulpo a la gallega
*Octopus Galician style.
Octopus cooked and*

served hot in olive oil.
They are seasoned with
substantial amounts of
paprika, and sea-salt for
texture and flavor.

Puntillitas *Battered and
fried tiny squid. Also
known as chopitos.*

Queso con anchoas
*Castilla or Manchego
cured cheese topped with
anchovies.*

Queso *variety of cheeses*

Rajo *Pork seasoned with
garlic and parsley. A
variety with added
paprika is called Zorza.*

**Salmon Ahumado con
Queso Blando** *Smoked
salmon with cream cheese*

Salsichon *mild Spanish
pork sausage*

Sepia *Cuttlefish, usually
grilled*

**Solomillo a la
castellana** *Fried pork
scallops, served with an
onion and/or Cabrales
cheese sauce*

**Solomillo al whisky, or
al güisqui** *Fried pork
scallops, marinated using
whisky, brandy or white
wine and olive oil.*

Tortilla de patatas
*Omelet containing fried
chunks of potatoes and
sometimes onion.*

Tortilla Española *Omelet
with potatoes and onion.
A variety containing
vegetables and chorizo
(similar to frittata)
is known as Tortilla
Paisana.*

Tortillitas de camarones
Battered-prawn fritters.

Zamburiñas *Zamburiñas
are a type of scallop,
which are often served
in a marinara, tomato-
based sauce.*

Spanish Food

A

A la parilla/plancha *grilled*

A la brasa *charcoal grilled*

A la romana *fried in batter*

Abulón *abalone*

Acedera *sorrel*

Aceite *oil*

Aceite girasol *sunflower oil*

Aceite de oliva *olive oil*

Aceituna *olive*

Aceitunas rellenas *stuffed olives*

Acelgas *chard*

Achicoria *chicory*

Aderezo *salad dressing*

Adobado *marinated*

Agachadiza *snipe (game bird)*

Agrazada *verjuice (juice from unripe, immature grapes)*

Agridulce *sweet and sour*

Agrio *sour*

Agrio/ácido *bitter*

Agua *water*

Agua de coco *coconut milk*

Aguacate *avocado*

Aguado *liquid*

Aguaturma *Jerusalem artichoke*

Aguayon *rump*

Agulat *Euro. fish, known as Rock Salmon*

Ahumado *smoked (fish or other)*

Ají *chili peppers*

Ajíaceite *garlic mayonnaise*

Ajo *garlic*

Ajoarriero *cod stew with red peppers*

Ajonjoli *sesame seeds*

Al ajillo *in garlic*

Alas *wings*

Albahaca *basil*

Albaricoques *apricots*

Albardilla *batter*

Albillos *white wine grapes*

Albóndiga *meatball (usu. pork)*

Albóndigas con guisantes *beef meatballs in tomato sauce with peas*

Albondiguillas *small meatballs*

Albondiguillas a la criolla *small meatballs in tomato-sweet pepper sauce with saffron rice*

Alcachofa *artichoke*

Alcachofas con jamón *artichokes with ham*

Alcachofas salteadas *sauté artichokes*

Alcachofas vinagreta *artichoke vinaigrette*

Alcaparras *capers*

Alcaravea *caraway seed*

Al horno *baked*

Al cuarto de hora *(15 minute soup) mussel soup with diced ham, onions, parsley and rice, garnished with chopped hard boiled eggs*

Alfóncigo *pistachio nut*

Alga *seaweed*

Aliñado *seasoned, flavored*

Aliño *seasoning, sometimes salad dressing*

Alioli *garlic mayonnaise*

Alitán *dogfish (shark)*

Almejas *clams*

Almejas a la marinera *clams stewed in wine and parsley*

Almejas naturales *live clams*

Almendras *almonds*

Almíbar *syrup*

Almuerzo *lunch*

Alubias con... *beans with...*

Alubias negras *black beans*

Alubias rojas *kidney beans*

Anchoa *anchovy*

Anémona de mar *sea anemone*

Angelote *angel fish*

Angola *soured milk*

Anguila (ahumada) *eel (smoked)*

Angulas *baby eels*

Añadir *add*

Añejo *beef from 14 month old cattle*

Anís *anisette*

Ancas de rana *frogs' legs*

Ansarino *young goose*

Apagar *turn off*

Apio *celery*

Apio-nabo *celeriac*

Aplanar *roll out*

Aplastar/aplanar *flatten*

Arándano (rojo y agrio) *cranberry*

Ardilla *squirrel*

Arenque *herring*

   -ahumado *smoked herring, kipper*

   -en escabeche *pickled herring*

   -marinados *marinated herring*

Arroces *rice dishes*

   -Caldosos *soggy, soupy rice*

   -Melosos *honeyed rice*

   -Secos *dry rice*

Arroz *rice*

   -a la alicantina *fish stew over rice, with garlic, artichoke hearts and saffron*

   -a la cubana *rice with fried eggs and banana fritters*

   -a la valenciana *rice with sea food*

   -blanco *white rice*

   -con leche *rice pudding*

   -negro *rice cooked in cuttlefish ink*

   -parillada *variety of meats (pork, chicken, sausage) fried with artichoke hearts and string beans and served with rice*

   -valenciana *rice with sweet peppers, chicken, ham and mushrooms in a tomato-based sauce*

Asado/asar *roast(ed)*

Asado de Carrilleras *roast hog jowl (pig's cheek)*

Asadura *entrails, offal*

Asar a la parrilla *to grill*

Aspic, galantina *aspic*

Atar *to tie*

Atún *tuna*

Avellanas *hazelnuts*
Avena *oats*
Azafrán *saffron*
Azucar *sugar*
Azúcar blanca de granulado muy fino *caster sugar*
Azúcar glace *icing sugar*

B

Bacalao *cod*
    -a la vizcaína *cod served with ham, peppers and chillis*
    -al pil pil *cod served with chillis and garlic*
    -salado *salt cod*
Barbacoa/parrillada *barbeque*
Barquillos *biscuits*
Barra *loaf*
Batido *milk shake*
    -de chocolate *chocolate milk shake*
    -de fresas *strawberry milk shake*
    -de frutas *fruit milk shake*
    -de vainilla *vanilla milk shake*
Batir *whisk*
Bebidas *drinks*
Bechamel *bechamel sauce*
Beicón *bacon*
Bellota *acorn*
Berberechos *cockles*
Berenjena *eggplant*
Berro *watercress*
Berza *cabbage*

Besugo *sea bream*
   -al horno *baked sea bream*
Betarraga *beetroot*
Bistec *steak*
   -de ternera *veal steak*
Bizcochos *sponge fingers, ladyfingers*
Bocadillo *sandwich on crusty roll*
Bogavante *lobster*
Bollo *bread roll*
Boqueróns *fresh anchovies in vinegar (a popular tapa)*
Boquerones fritos *fried anchovies*
Boniato, batata, camote *sweet potato*
Bonito *tuna*
Borde *edge*
Borraja *borage*
Botella *bottle*
Brevas *figs*
Brócoli, brécol *broccoli*
Broqueta de riñones *kidney kebabs*
Brotes de soja *soybean sprouts*
Budín, pudín, pudding; (postre) *pudding*
Buñuelos *light fried pastries, fritters*
Bunuelos de Bacalao *cod fritters*
Butifarra *Catalan sausage*

C

Caballa *mackerel*
Cabrito *kid goat*
   -asado *roast kid*

S

Cachelada *pork stew with eggs tomato and onion*

Cafe *coffee*

  -americano *as espresso but with much more water so bigger and weaker*

  -con hielo *coffee with ice*

  -con leche *coffee with plenty of milk, hot or cold*

  -cortado *espresso with a drop of milk*

Cafe solo *black espresso*

Calabacín,calabacita *zucchini*

Calabaza *marrow*

Calabaza (peru) zapallo *pumpkin*

Calamar, calamares *squid*

Calamares a la romana *squid rings in batter*

Calamares en su tinta *squid cooked in their ink*

Calamares fritos *fried squid*

Caldeirada *fish soup*

Caldereta gallega *vegetable stew*

Caldo *stock, broth*

Caldo de... *...soup*

  -de gallina *chicken soup*

  -de pescado *clear soup made with fish*

  -gallego *vegetable soup*

  -guanche *soup made with potatoes onions tomatoes and courgettes/squash*

Calentar *warm*

Callos *tripe*

  -a la madrileña *tripe cooked with chillis*

Camaron *prawn*

Camarones *baby prawns*

Canela *cinnamon*

C

Canelones *cannelloni*

Cangrejo *crab*

Cangrejos de río *river crab*

Capa *layer*

Caraco, caracoles *snail*

**Caramelo duro hecho con azúcar y
   mantequilla** *butterscotch*

Carne *meat*

  -de buey *beef*

  -de pecho *brisket*

  -de Res *Beef*

  -de ternera *veal*

  -de vaca *beef*

  -de salchicha *sausage meat*

  -en salsa *meat in tomato sauce*

  -picada *minced meat*

C

Carrilladas *cow's cheeks*

Carrilleras *hog jowl (pig's cheek)*

Carro de queso *cheese board*

Cáscara *rind*

Cáscaras *shells*

Caseras *homemade*

Castañas , Castaño *chestnut*

Cazo *saucepan*

Cazón *dogfish, shark*

Cebolla *onion*

Cebolleta *shallot*

Cebolleta, cebollín, cebolla de verdeo *scallion
   (young onion)*

Cena *dinner*

Cenina *thinly-sliced, dry-cured beef*

Centollo *spider crab*

Centro de esadilla *blade steak*

Cepillar *brush*

Cerdo *pork*

   -**picado** *minced pork*

Cerezas *cherries*

Cerveza *beer*

Cesta de frutas *basket of fresh fruit*

Chalote, chalota *shallot*

Chambarete *round steak*

Chambarete de mano *hind shank*

Chamorros *shank*

Champiñones *mushrooms*

Champiñón a la crema *mushrooms with cream sauce*

   -**al ajillo** *garlic mushrooms*

   -**salteado** *sauté mushrooms*

   -**a la plancha** *grilled mushrooms*

Chanquetes *fish (similar to whitebait)*

Chateaubrian *chateaubriand steak*

Chícharo (méxican) *peas*

Chicharrones *cracklings*

Chipirones *squid*

   -**en su tinta** *squid cooked in their ink*

   -**rellenos** *stuffed squid*

Chirimoyas *custard apples*

Chive (hierba) *chive (herb)*

Chocos *squid*

Chocolate *chocolate*

C

Chorizo *spanish chorizo sausage*
Chorrear un poco *trickle*
Chorrito *dash*
Chuleta de dos lomos *porterhouse steak*
Chuleta(s) *chop(s)*
  -**de buey** *beef chop*
  -**de cerdo empanada** *breaded pork chop*
  -**de cerdo** *pork chop*
  -**de cordero** *lamb chop*
  -**de cordero empanadas** *breaded lamb chop*
  -**de lomo ahumado** *smoked pork chop*
  -**de ternera empanada** *breaded veal chop*
  -**de ternera** *veal chop*
Chuletitas de cordero *small lamb chops*
Chuletón de buey *large beef chop, steak*
Chuletón *large chop*
Churros *deep fried tubes of dough covered in sugar. Eaten for breakfast, with hot chocolate*
Cigalas *king prawns*
Cigalas cocidas *boiled crayfish*
Cilantro, culantro *coriander*
Ciruela *plum*
Ciruelas pasas *prunes*
Ciruela (seca) *prune*
Clara de huevo *egg white*
Clavo (de olor) *clove*
Cocer al horno *bake*
Cochinillo *suckling pig*
Cochinillo asado *roast suckling pig*

Cocido Madrileño *stew with meat, Spanish sausage and chickpeas*

Cocido *stew*

Cocinar *cook*

Cocinar a fuego lento *simmer*

Coco *coconut*

Cocochas (de merluza) *cheeks of hake*

Cocoa (en polvo) *cocoa powder*

Cóctel de bogavante *hake stew*

Cóctel de gambas *prawn cocktail*

Cóctel de langostinos *king prawn cocktail*

Cóctel de mariscos *seafood cocktail*

Codornices *quail*

   -asadas *roasted quail*

   -con uvas *quail cooked with grapes*

   -escabechadas *marinated quail*

   -estofadas *braised quail*

Codorniz *quail*

Cogollo *heart (of cabbage, lettuce)*

Col *cabbage*

Colar-strain

Coles de bruselas *brussel sprouts*

   -salteadas *sauté Brussels sprouts*

Coliflor *cauliflower*

   -con bechamel *cauliflower with béchamel sauce and cheese*

Colorante alimenticio *food coloring*

Combinar *combine*

Comedor *dining room*

Comida *food*

Comida basura, porquerías *junk food*
Comidas *lunch*
Comilona *a nosh up*
Comino *cumin*
Comiso *packed lunch*
Completamente *thoroughly*
Concha *clam*
Condimento *seasoning*
Conejo *rabbit*
   -asado *roast rabbit*
   -encebollado *rabbit served with onions*
   -estofado *braised rabbit*
Congelado *frozen*
Congrio *conger eel*
Conservante *preservative*
Conservar *preserve*
Consistencia *consistency*
Coñac *brandy*
Consomé *comsommé (strained broth)*
   -al jerez *consommé with sherry*
   -con yema *consommé with egg yolk*
   -de ave *chicken consommé*
   -de pollo *chicken consommé*
Contra de ternera con guisantes *veal stew with peas*
Contra filete de ternera *veal fillet*
Copa ... *... cup or glass*
Copa de helado *ice cream scoop*
Copos de avena *oats*
Copos de maíz tostados *cornflakes*

Corazon *heart*

Corazones de alcachofas *hearts of artichoke*

Corazón de cordero *lamb's heart*

Cordero, Cordera *lamb*

   -asado *roast lamb*

Cordero chilindron *lamb stew with onion, tomato, peppers and eggs*

Cortado en cuatro *quartered*

Cortar *trim*

Cortar en cuadritos *diced*

Cortar en lonchas finas *thinly slice*

Cosa para pelar patatas *potato peeler*

Costillas *ribs*

Costillas *spare ribs*

Crema agria *sour cream*

Crema dulce *sweet cream*

Crema para batir *whipping cream*

Crema pastelero *confectioner's custard*

Crepe *pancake*

Criadillas *testicles, beef or lamb, usually breaded and fried in oil*

Croqueta *an oval of potato, flour, egg and often chopped meat coated with breadcrumbs and deep-fried*

Crudo *raw*

Crujiente, crocante *crispy*

Cuajar *curdle*

Cuajo *rennet*

Cubrir *cover*

Cuchara (grande o de servir) *tablespoon*

Cuchara de medir *measuring spoon*

S

Cucharada *spoon*
Cucharita, cucharilla *teaspoon*
Cucharones *ladles*
Cuchillo *knife*
Cuenco *bowls*
Cuscurro *crouton*

D

Dar la vuelta *turn*
Dátiles *dates*
De grano grueso *coarse*
De horno *ovenproof*
Dehuesado *boned*
Dejar en adobo, marinar *marinade, marinate*
Delicias *delights, referring to assorted desserts*
De la casa *of the house*
Derretido *melted*
Derretir *melt*
Desayuno, desayunar *breakfast*
Descansar *rest*
Deshuesado *boned, boneless*
Despensa *larder*
Dientes de ajo *cloves of garlic*
Dividir en dos *halve*
Doblar *fold*
Donut, rosquilla *doughnut*
Dorado *golden, mahi mahi*
Dorar *v. Brown*
Dulce *sweet*
Dulce de membrillo *quince jelly and cheese*

E

Embutido *sausage*

Embutidos *selection of cold sausages*

Empanada, (empanadilla) *fish, meat filled pie (smaller version)*

   -gallega *tuna fish pastry*

   -santiaguesa *tuna fish pastry*

   -de bonito *tuna pastry*

   -de carne *meat pastrys*

   -de chorizo *Spanish sausage pastry*

Emperador *Swordfish*

En lata *tinned*

En trozos *sliced*

En trozos menudos *finely chopped*

En vez de *instead of*

Encender *light*

Enchilada *mexican tortilla with a meat or cheese filling, served with a tomato and chili sauce*

Endibias *endives*

Endivia, achicoria *chicory*

Endulzante *sweetener*

Endulzar, azucarar *sweeten*

Eneldo *dill*

Enfriar *chill*

Engrasado *greased*

Engrasar *oil*

En salsa *in sauce*

Ensaimada mallorquina *Majorca cake*

Ensalada *salad*

   -de arenque *herring salad*

-**de atún** *tuna salad*

-**de frutas** *salad with fruit*

-**de gambas** *prawn salad*

-**de lechuga** *simple green salad*

-**de pollo** *chicken salad*

-**de tomate** *tomato salad*

-**ilustrada** *mixed salad: (tomato, lettuce & onion)*

-**mixta** *mixed salad (tomato, lettuce & onion)*

-**simple** *simple green salad*

Ensaladilla *Russian salad (mayonnaise salad with potatoes, carrots and peas)*

Ensaladilla rusa *see ensaladilla*

Entero *whole*

Entrecot a la parrilla *grilled entrecot steak*

Entrecot de ternera *veal entrecot steak*

Entremeses de la casa *homemade hors d'oeuvres*

Entremeses variados *hors d'oeuvres*

Escaldar *scald*

Escalfado *poached*

Escalope a la parrilla *grilled veal*

Escalope a la milanesa *breaded veal escalope with cheese*

Escalope a la plancha *grilled veal escalope*

Escalope de lomo de cerdo *escalope of fillet of pork*

Escalope de ternera *veal escalope*

Escalope empanado *breaded escalope*

Escalopines al vino de Marsala *veal escalopes cooked in wine*

Escalopines de ternera *small veal escalopes*

Escarola *curly endive*

Escurrir *drain*

Espadilla *shoulder chop*

Espadín a la toledana *kebab*

Espaguetis *spaghetti*

Espaguetis italiana *spaghetti*

Espárrago *asparagus*
   -con mayonesa *asparagus with mayonnaise*

Espesar *thicken*

Espeso *stiff*

Espesura, grueso *thickness*

Espinacas *spinach*
   -a la crema *spinach in cream sauce*

Espinazo de cerdo con patatas *stew of pork ribs with potatoes*

Espuma *foam*

Espumadera *slotted spoon*

Estofado *casserole, stew*
   -de liebre *jugged hare*

Estragón *tarragon*

Exprimir *squeeze*

F

F

Fabada *asturian casserole of beans, chorizo, morcilla and pancetta*

Faisán *pheasant*
   -con castañas *pheasant with chestnuts*
   -estofado *stewed pheasant*
   -trufado *pheasant with truffles*

Fécula *potato starch*

Fiambres *cold meats*

Fideos *small noodles*
Filetes *fillets*
   -a la parrilla *grilled beef*
   -de cerdo *pork steak*
   -de ternera *veal steak*
Flan *caramel custard*
   -al ron *caramel custard with rum*
   -de caramelo *caramel custard*
Formas *shapes*
Freír *fry*
Fresa *strawberry*
Fresas con nata *strawberries with cream*
Frigorífico *fridge*
Frijol *lima bean*
Frijoles refritos *refried beans*
Frito *fried*
Fritura de Pescados *fish fry*
Frotar *rub*
Fruta *fruit*
   -en almíbar *fruit in syrup*
Fruta variada *assorted fresh fruit*
Fuego fuerte *high heat*

G

Gallena *hen*
Galleta *cookie*
Galleta salada (generalmente en forma de 8) *pretzel*
Gallina en pepitoria *chicken stewed with peppers*
Gallinejas *fried lamb's intestines*

Gambas *prawns*
  -**a la plancha** *grilled prawns*
  -**al ajillo** *garlic prawns*
  -**cocidas** *boiled prawns*
  -**con mayonesa** *prawns with mayonnaise*
  -**en gabardina** *prawns in batter*
  -**rebozadas** *prawns in batter*
Gancho de carnicero *meathook*
Garbanzos *chick peas*
  -**a la catalana** *chickpeas with sausage, boiled eggs and pine nuts*
Gazpacho *cold tomato soup*
Gelatina *gelatine*
Gelatina *jelly*
Goloso *sweet toothed*
Granada *pomegranate*
Granos de pimienta *peppercorns*
Grasa *grease*
Gratén de ... *... au gratin*
Gratinar *grill*
Grisín, colín *bread stick*
Grueso, espeso *thick*
Guarnición *garnish*
Guayaba *guava*
Guisado *casserole*
Guisantes *peas*
  -**con jamón** *peas with ham*
  -**salteadas** *sauté peas*
Guiso de fideos con bacalao *cod stew with noodles*

H

Habas *broad beans*
Habas/habichuelas/alubias/frijol *beans*
   -con jamón *ham and broad beans*
   -fritas *fried young broad beans*
Habichuelas ejote *green beans*
Hacer puré *mash*
Harina *flour*
Harina de maíz *cornflour*
Helado *ice cream*
   -de caramelo *caramel ice cream*
   -de chocolate *chocolate ice cream*
   -de fresa *strawberry ice cream*
   -de mantecado *vanilla ice cream*
   -de nata *plain ice cream*
   -de vainilla *vanilla ice cream*

Hervido *stew*
Hervir *boil*
Hierba *herb*
Hierba doncella *myrtle (ame), periwinkle (bre)*
Hierbabuena *mint*
Hierbaluisa *lemon verbena*
Hígado *liver*
   -con cebolla *liver cooked with onions*
   -de ternera estofado *braised liver of veal*
   -estofado *braised liver*
Higo *fig*
Higo chumbo *prickly pear*
Higos con miel y nueces *figs with honey and nuts*
Higos secos *dried figs*

Hinojo *fennel*

Hoja *leaf*

Hoja del cuchillo *blade of a knife*

Hojaldre *puff pastry*

Hojas *leaves, salad greens*

Hongos *mushrooms*

Horchata (de chufas) *cold almond-flavoured milk drink*

Horno *oven*

Huachinango *red snapper*

Hueco *dent*

Hueso/espina *bone*

Hueva *roe*

Huevera *eggcup*

Huevo(s) *egg(s)*

   -**duro** *hard boiled egg*

   -**hilado** *egg yolk garnish*

   -**a la flamenca** *fried eggs with hamtomato and vegetables*

   -**cocidos** *hard boiled eggs*

   -**con jamón** *eggs with cured ham*

   -**con mayonesa** *boiled eggs with mayonnaise*

   -**con panceta** *eggs with bacon*

   -**con patatas fritas** *fried eggs and chips (fries)*

   -**con picadillo** *eggs with minced Spanish sausage*

   -**con salchichas** *eggs and sausages*

   -**escalfados** *poached eggs*

   -**fritos con chorizo** *fried eggs with Spanish sausage*

   -**fritos con jamón** *fried eggs with cured ham*

-fritos *fried eggs*
-pasados por agua *soft-boiled eggs*
-rellenos *stuffed eggs*
-revuelto con tomate *scrambled eggs with tomato*
-revueltos *scrambled eggs*

I

Importado *imported (often used for liquors)*
Ingredientes *ingredients*

J

Jabalí *wild boar*
Jaiba *crab*
Jamón *ham*
-con huevo hilado *ham with egg yolk garnish*
-de Jabugo *excellent quality Spanish cured ham*
-de Trevélez *good quality Spanish cured ham*
-serrano *Spanish cured ham*
-york *cooked ham*
Jarra graduada *measuring jug*
Jerez *sherry*
-amontillado *pale dry sherry*
-fino *pale light sherry*
-oloroso *sweet sherry*
Jeta *pork cheek*
Jocoque *buttermilk*
Judías verdes *French beans*
-a la española *bean stew*
-al natural *plain French beans*

-con jamón *French beans with cured ham*
Jugo/zumo *juice*
  -de albaricoque *apricot juice*
  -de limón *lemon juice*
  -de lima *lime juice*
  -de melocotón *peach juice*
  -de naranja *orange juice*
  -de piña *pineapple juice*
  -de tomate *tomato juice*
Jugoso *juicy*
Juliana *julienne*
Jumilla *light mistela wines from Murcia*
Jurel *yellow tail*

K

Kilo *a kilogram (approx. 2.2 lbs)*

L

Lado *side*
Langosta *rock lobster*
Langosta a la americana *lobster with brandy and garlic*
Langosta a la catalana *lobster with mushrooms and ham in béchamel sauce*
Langosta fría con mayonesa *cold lobster with mayonnaise*
Langosta gratinada *lobster au gratin*
Langostinas *king prawns*
Lata *can*
Lata *tin*

Laurel *bayleaf*
Lavar *wash*
Lean ‹ *meat* › *magro, sin grasa*
Leche *milk*
Leche cuajada *junket*
Leche frita *pudding with milk and eggs*
Leche merengada *cold milk with meringues*
Lechoso *milky (con mucha leche)*
Lechuga *lettuce*
Lechón (cochinillo) *suckling pig*
Lengua *tongue beef, veal, pork, lamb are used*
Lengua de buey *ox tongue*
Lenguado *sole, flounder*
  -a la parrilla *grilled sole*
  -a la plancha *grilled sole*
  -a la romana *battered sole*
  -frito *fried sole*
  -grillado *grilled sole*
  -meuniere *sole meuniere*

Lengue de cordero estofada *stewed lamb tongue*
Lentamente *gradually*
Lentejas *lentils*
Lentejas aliñadas *lentils with vinaigrette*
Levadura (en polvo) *baking powder*
Liebre *hare*
Liebre estofada *stewed hare*
Lima *lime*
Limón *lemon*
Limpiar con agua *rinse*
Limpiar con un paño *wipe*

Lisa *striped mullet*
Lista de la compra *shopping list*
Lombarda rellena *stuffed red cabbage*
Lombarda salteada *sauté red cabbage*
Lo que se pone encima de una base *topping*
Lomo *pork loin*
   -**curado** *cured pork sausage*
   -**de cerdo** *tenderloin*
Lomo de Buey a la Parrilla *grilled beef tenderloin*
Loncha *slice*
Lubina *sea bass*

M

Macarrones *macaroni*
Macarrones gratinados *macaroni & cheese*
Macedonia de fruta *fruit salad (desert)*
Machacar *grind*
Maduro *ripe*
Magdalena *cupcake*
Magret de Pato *duck breast*
Magro *lean (meat)*
Mahonesa *mayonnaise*
Maíz tierno *sweetcorn*
Málaga *sweet wine*
Mandarinas *tangerines*
Manises *peanuts*
Manitas *pig's feet*
Manitas de cordero *lamb shank*
Manos de cerdo a la parrilla *grilled pigs' trotters*
Manos de cerdo *pigs' trotters*

S

M

Manteca, grasa de cerdo *lard*
Mantecadas *small sponge cakes*
Mantequilla *butter*
Manteca de res *suet*
Manzana *apple*
Manzanas asadas *baked apples*
Manzanilla *dry sherry-type drink*
Mariscada *cold mixed shellfish*
Mariscos *shellfish*
  -del día *fresh shellfish*
  -del tiempo *seasonal shellfish*
Masa *dough*
Masa horneada *yorkshire pudding*
Macerado *marinated*
Mayonesa *mayonnaise*
Mazapán *marzipan*
Medallones *medallions (small steaks)*
  -de anguila *eel steaks*
  -de merluza *hake steaks*
Media de agua *half-bottle of mineral water*
Mejillón cebra *zebra mussel*
Mejillones *mussels*
  -a la marinera *mussels in wine sauce*
Melaza *molasses*
Melocotón, durazno *peach*
  -en almíbar *peaches in syrup*
Melón *melon*
Melón (de pulpa verdosa muy dulce) *honeydew melon*
Melón con jamón *melon with cured ham*

Membrillo *quince*
Menú de la casa *fixed price menu*
Menú del día *fixed price menu*
Menudencias *Organs, giblets*
Menestra de legumbres *vegetable stew*
Menestra de verduras *mixed vegetables*
Menta *mint*
Menudencias *giblets*
Menú de la casa *fixed price menu*
Menú del día *fixed price menu*
Merluza *hake*
  -**a la cazuela** *stewed hake*
  -**a la parrilla** *grilled hake*
  -**a la plancha** *grilled hake*
  -**a la riojana** *hake with chilis*
  -**a la romana** *hake steaks in batter*
  -**a la vasca** *hake in a garlic sauce*
  -**al ajo arriero** *hake with garlic and chilis*
  -**en salsa verde** *hake in a parsley and wine sauce*
  -**en salsa** *hake in sauce*
  -**fría** *cold hake*
  -**frita** *fried hake*
Mermelada *marmalade*
  -**de albaricoque** *apricot jam*
  -**de ciruelas** *prune jam*
  -**de frambuesas** *raspberry jam*
  -**de fresas** *strawberry jam*
  -**de limón** *lemon marmalade*
  -**de melocotón** *peach jam*
  -**de naranja** *orange marmalade*

M

S

Mero *grouper, sea bass*
- **a la parrilla** *grilled grouper*
- **en salsa verde** *grouper with garlic and parsley sauce*

Mesa *table*
Mezclar *mix*
Miel *honey*
Migas de pan/pan rallado *breadcrumbs*
Milanesa *cutlet*
Mojama *salt-cured tuna, dried or smoked*
Mojarra *sunfish, bluegill*
Molido, pulverizado *ground*
Mollejas, lechecillas *sweetbreads*
Mollejas de ternera fritas *fried sweetbreads*
Mollete *muffin*
Mora *blackberry*
Morcilla *black pudding, blood pudding*
Morcilla de carnero *black pudding made from mutton*
Morcón *blood sausage*
Morros *cheeks*
Morros *cheeks, jowls*
- **de cerdo** *pigs' cheeks*
- **de vaca** *beef cheek*

Morteruelo *type of mince pie*
Mortero *mortar*
Mostaza *mustard*
Mousse de ... *... mousse*
Mousse de chocolate *chocolate mousse*
Mousse de limón *lemon mousse*

M

Muslo de pollo *drumstick (chicken)*

N

Nabos *turnips*
Naranja *orange*
Nata *cream*
Nata agria *sour cream*
Nata montada *whipped cream*
Natilla *custard*
Natillas de chocolate *custard with chocolate*
Navajas *razor clams*
Nectarina *nectarine*
Níscalos *wild mushrooms*
Nispero *the fruit of a small deciduous tree of the rose family. It resembles a crab apple and is eaten fresh and used in preserves*
No engordante *non fattening*
Nueces (de california) *walnuts*
Nuez (nueces) *nut, (nuts)*
Nuez de mantequilla *knob of butter*
Nuez moscada *nutmeg*
Nutritivo *nourishing*

O

Oca *goose*
Onza (28.35 gramos) *ounce*
Orégano *oregano*
Oreja (de cerdo) *pigs' ears*
Orujo *spirit obtained from grape musts*
Ostras, osteon *oysters*

P

Paella *rice with chicken and seafood*
Paella castellana *fried rice with meat*
Paleta de cordero lechal *shoulder of lamb*
Palitos de queso *cheese straws*
Paloma *pigeon or dove*
Pampano *pompano*
Pan *bread*
   -ázimo, pan sin levadura *unleavened (bread)*
   -de molde *sliced bread*
   -duro *stale bread*
   -integral *brown bread*
Panache de verduras *vegetable stew*
Panceta *fatty pork or streaky bacon*
Panera (para guardar el pan) *breadbin*
Papel de cocina *kitchen tissue*
Pargo *snapper*
Parrillada de caza *mixed grilled game*
Parrillada de mariscos *mixed grilled shellfish*
Pasa (de uva) *raisin*
Pasta *pasta*
Pastel *cake*
Pastel de ternera *veal pie*
Pasteles *cakes*
Patatas *potatoes*
   -a la pescadora *potatoes with fish*
   -a lo pobre *fried potatoes with greens*
   -alioli *potatoes in garlic mayonnaise*
   -asadas *roast potatoes*
   -bravas *deep fried potatoes in spicy sauce*

-fritas *french fries*
Patitos rellenos *stuffed duckling*
Pato *duck*
  -asado *roast duck*
  -estofado *stewed duck*
Pavipollo *large chicken*
Pavo *turkey*
  -asado *roast turkey*
  -relleno *stuffed turkey*
  -trufado *turkey stuffed with truffles*
Pechuga de pollo *chicken breast*
Pedazo grande *wedge*
Pelado *peeled, skinned*
Pelar *peel*
Pepinillo *gherkins*
Pepino *cucumber*
Pepitas (trocitos) de pollo *chicken nuggets*

Pera *pear*
Percebes *goose barnacle*
Perdices *partridges*
  -a la campesina *partridges with vegetables*
  -a la manchega *partridges in red wine with garlic, herbs & pepper*
  -asadas *roast partridges*
  -con chocolate *partridges with chocolate*
  -escabachadas *marinated partridges*
Perdiz *partridge*
Perejil *parsley*
Perro or perrito caliente, pancho *hot dog*
Pescadilla *whiting*

Pescaditos *whitebait*
   -**fritos** *fried fish (whitebait)*
Pescado *fish*
Pescado blanco *whitefish*
Pestiños *fried fish*
Pez espada *swordfish*
   -**ahumado** *smoked swordfish*
Picadillo de ternera *minced veal*
Picante *spicy*
Picar *chop*
Pichon *pigeon*
Piel/pelar *skin*
Pierna *leg*
Pierna deshuesada *boneless leg*
Pimentón *paprika*

Pimienta *pepper ie peppercorns*
Pimienta cayena *cayenne pepper*
Pimientas rellenas *stuffed peppers*
Pimientos a la riojana *baked red peppers fried in oil and garlic*
Pimientos fritos *fried peppers*
Pimientos rellenos *stuffed peppers*
Pimiento rojo *red pepper*
Pimiento verde *green pepper*
Piña *pineapple*
   -**al gratin** *pineapple au gratin*
   -**fresca** *fresh pineapple*
Pinchitos *snacks served in bars*
Pincho moruno *kebab*
Piñones *pinenuts, pignolia*

Pisto *fried mixed vegetables*

Pisto manchego *ratatouille (braised sweet pepper and eggplant stew)*

Pizca *pinch*

Pizza *pizza*

Plátano *banana*

Platanos flameandos *flambé bananas*

Plato *dish*

Platos combinados *mixed plate (eg, chips, eggs, sausage and black pudding)*

Plato principal, segundo plato *main course*

Pochar *fry ... Until soft*

Polen de Abejas *bee pollen*

Pollo *chicken*

    -a la ajillo *fried chicken with garlic*

    -a la champaña *chicken au champagne*

    -a la parrilla *grilled chicken*

    -a la riojana *chicken with peppers and chilis*

    -a la vino blanco *chicken in white wine*

    -asado *roast chicken*

    -braseado *braised chicken*

    -con tomate *chicken with tomatoes*

    -con verduras *chicken and vegetables*

    -en cacerola *chicken casserole*

    -en pepitoria *chicken in wine with saffrongarlic and almonds*

    -salteado *chicken sauté*

    -de leche *fryer*

Polverones *Christmas sweet*

Pomelo *grapefruit*

Poner *arrange*
Poner trocitos encima *dot with*
Popietas *rollups*
Porras *like churros, but thicker, and more doughy*
Postre *dessert*
Potaje castellano *thick broth*
Potaje de garbanzos *chickpea stew*
Potaje de habichuelas *white bean stew*
Potaje de lentejas *lentil stew*
Productos alimenticios, comestibles *foodstuffs*
Puchero canario *casserole containing chickpeas and corn*
Puerros *leeks*
Pulpitos con cebolla *baby octopus with onions*
Pulpo *octopus*
Puntillas *baby squid*
Punto de ebullición *boiling point*
Punto de fusión *melting point*
Puñado *handful*
Puré *purée*
Puré de patatas *mashed potato*
Purrasalda *cod with leeks and potatoes*

Q

Queso *cheese*
  -**con membrillo** *cheese with quince jelly*
  -**de Burgos** *soft white cheese*
  -**de bola** *Dutch cheese*
  -**de oveja** *sheep's cheese*
  -**del pais** *local cheese*

-gallego *creamy cheese*
Quisquillas *shrimps*
Quitar *get rid of, remove*

R

Rábano *radish*
Rabo de buey *oxtail*
Ragout de ternera *veal ragout (stew)*
Rallado *grated*
Ramita *sprig*
Rape *monkfish*
   -a la americana *monk fish with brandy and herbs*
   -a la cazuela *monk fish stew*
   -a la plancha *grilled monk fish*
Raviolis *ravioli*
Raya *skate*
Rebozar *coat*
Receta *recipe*
Recetario *recipe book*
Redondo al horno *roast fillet of beef*
Reducir *reduce*
Refresco (bebida no alcohólica) *soft drink*
Rellenar *stuff*
Relleno *filling*
Rellenos *stuffed*
Reloj de arena *egg timer*
Remojar *soak*
Remojon *cod with orange and olives*
Remolacha *beetroot*
Rennina *rennin*

Repollo *cabbage*
Repostería de la casa *cakes baked on the premises*
Requeson *cream cheese/cottage cheese*
Revuelto *scrambled egg*
   -de ajos tiernos *scrambled egg with spring garlic*
   -de angulas *scrambled egg with baby eels*
   -de gambas *scrambled egg with prawns*
   -de sesos *scrambled egg with brains*
   -de trigueros *scrambled egg with asparagus*
   -mixto *scrambled eggs with mixed vegetables*
Ribeiro *white wine from Galicia*
Rioja *good wine from Logroño*
Riñon *kidney*
Riñones al jerez *kidneys with sherry*
Robalo *snook*

Rociando *basting*
Rodaballo *turbot (fish)*
Rollito *roll*
Romero *rosemary*
Ron *rum*
Rosbi *roast beef*
Roscas *sweet pastries*

S

Sabor *taste*
Sacar con cuchara *spoon*
Sal *salt*
Salado *salted*
Salchicha *sausage*
   -de Frankfurt *Frankfurter sausages*

-envuelta en hojaldre *sausage roll*

Salchichón *white sausage with pepper*

Salmón *salmon*

  -a la parrilla *grilled salmon*

  -ahumado *smoked salmon*

  -frio *cold salmon*

Salmonete *red mullet*

  -a la parrilla *grilled red mullet*

  -en papillote *red mullet cooked in foil*

Salmorejo *cold vegetable soup*

Salmpimentar *season with salt and pepper*

Salpicar *sprinkle*

Salpicón de mariscos *shellfish with vinaigrette*

Salsa *sauce*

  -allioli (or ali oli) *mayonnaise with garlic*

  -bechamel *white sauce*

  -de soja *soy sauce*

  -hecha a base de miga de pan y leche *bread sauce*

  -holandesa *Hollandaise (egg yolk, butter and lemon)*

  -tártara *tartar sauce*

Salteadas con *sauteed with*

Saltear *sauté*

Salvaje *wild*

Sandía *watermelon*

Sandwichera *sandwich toaster*

Sangría *mixture of red wine, lemonade, spirits and fruit*

Sangre *congealed blood (fried with garlic)*

Sardinas *sardines*
- **-a la brasa** *barbecued sardines*
- **-a la parrilla** *grilled sardines*
- **-ahumadas** *smoked sardines*
- **-fritas** *fried sardines*

Sartén *frying pan*

Sazonar *season with salt*

Secar, Seco *dry*

Sellar *seal*

Semidulce *medium sweet*

Semillas *seeds*

Sepia *cuttlefish*

Sesos *brains*
- **-a la romana** *fried (lamb's) brains in batter*
- **-rebozados** *brains in batter*

Setas *mushrooms*
- **-a la plancha** *grilled mushrooms*
- **-rellanas** *stuffed mushrooms*

Sidra *cider*

Sierra *Spanish mackerel*

Sofreír *to sauté, fry lightly*

Sofrito *lightly fried*

Solomillo *Porterhouse steak*
- **-con guisantes** *fillet steak with peas*
- **-con patatas** *steak with potatoes*
- **-de ternera** *fillet of veal*
- **-de vaca** *fillet of beef*
- **-frio** *cold roast beef*

Sopa *soup*
- **-castellana** *vegetable soup*

S

-**de ajo** *garlic soup*

-**de almendros** *almond-based pudding*

-**de cocido** *meat soup (very watery)*

-**de cola de buey** *ox-tail soup*

-**de fideos** *noodle soup*

-**de gallina** *chicken soup*

-**de legumbres** *vegetable soup*

-**de lentejas** *lentil soup*

-**de mariscos** *seafood soup*

-**de pescado** *fish soup*

-**de rabo de buey** *ox-tail soup*

-**del dia** *soup of the day*

-**mallorquina** *soup with tomatomeat and eggs*

-**sevillana** *fish and mayonnaise soup*

Sorbete *sorbet*

Soufflé *soufflé*

-**de fresones** *strawberry soufflé*

-**de naranja** *orange soufflé*

-**de queso** *cheese soufflé Suero (de la leche) buttermilk*

Sumergir *dip*

Suplemento de verduras *extra vegetables*

Surtidos *assorted, assortment*

T

Taberna *tavern*

Tabla de cortar el pan *breadboard*

Tallarines *noodles*

Tallarines a la italiano *tagliatelle*

Tallo *stalk*

Tamale *(ground maize and sometimes meat or a sweet filling. Wrapped in a banana or maize leaf)-tamal*

Tamizar *sieve*

Tapadera *lid*

Tarta *tart (pastry)*

   -**de almendra** *almond tart*

   -**de chocolate** *chocolate tart*

   -**de fresas** *strawberry tart*

   -**de helado** *ice cream gateau*

   -**de la casa** *tart baked on the premises*

   -**de manzana** *apple tart*

   -**mocca** *mocha tart*

   -**de queso** *cheesecake*

Tartaleta sablé *shortbread tart*

Taza para medir *measuring cup*

Tencas *tench*

Tenedor *fork*

Ternera *veal*

   -**asada** *roast veal*

   -**picada** *minced veal*

Tiburon/cazon *shark*

Tibio *tepid*

Tierno *tender*

Tiritas *strips*

Tocinillos de cielo *creme caramel*

Tocino *pork fat*

Tocino entreverado *streaky bacon*

Tofu, queso de soja *tofu*

Tomates *tomatoes*

Tomates rellenos *stuffed tomatoes*

Tomatitos *tomatoes*

Tomillo *thyme*

Tordo *thrush*

Torrija, torreja, tostada que se vende en paquetes, biscote *french toast*

Tortilla *omelette*

   -a la paisana *omelette containing different vegetables*

   -a su gusto *omelette made to the customer's wishes*

   -alaska *Baked Alaska (dessert)*

   -de bonito *tuna fish omelette*

   -de champiñones *mushroom omelette*

   -de chorizo *omelette containing Spanish sausage*

   -de escabeche *fish omelette*

   -de esparragos *asparagus omelette*

   -de gambas *prawn omelette*

   -de jamón *cured ham omelette*

   -de patatas *spanish omelet*

   -de sesos *omelet with sheep's brains*

   -de setas *mushroom omelet*

   -española *Spanish potato omelet*

   -francesa *plain omelet*

   -sacramonte *vegetables, lamb's brains and testicles or sausage omelet*

   -variadas *various omelets*

Tortilla *(mexican) unleaved bread used to put food in*

Tostado *toasted*

Tournedó *beef fillet*

Transferir *transfer*
Triturar *make liquid*
Trucha *trout*
Trucha ahumada smoked trout
Trucha con jamón *trout with cured ham*
Trucha escabechada *marinated trout*
Truchas a la marinera *trout in wine sauce*
Truchas molinera *trout meuniere*
Trufa(s) *truffle(s)*
Trufa de chocolate *chocolate truffle*
Tulipa *serving dish, similar to ice cream sundae dish*
Turrón *nougat*
   -de Alicante *hard nougat*
   -de Jijona *soft nougat*
   -de coco *coconut nougat*
   -de yema *nougat with egg yolk*

U

U

Untar *smear*
Untar con mantequilla *butter*
Uvas *grapes*
Uvre de vaca *cow's udder*

V

Vaciar *empty*
Valdepeñas *fruity red wines from Valdepeñas*
Vapor *steamer*
Vaso *glass*
Venado *venison*
Ventresca *tuna belly meat*

Verduras *green vegetables*
Verter *pour*
Vieiras *scallops*
Vinagre *vinegar*
Vino blanco *white wine*
Vino de mesa *table wine*
Vino rosado *rosé wine*
Vino tinto *red wine*
Vodka *vodka*
Volver *return*

Whisky *whiskey*

Yema de huevo *egg yolk*
Yemas *yolks*

V

Zanahoria *carrot*
Zanahorias a la crema *carrots in cream sauce*
Zapallito *zucchini*
Zarajos *fried lamb's intestines*
Zarzuela *Seafood stew*
Zarzuela de mariscos *Seafood casserole*
Zumo de ... *... juice*
Zumo de albaricoque *apricot juice*
Zumo de limón *lemon juice*
Zumo de lima *lime juice*
Zumo de melocotón *peach juice*
Zumo de naranja *orange juice*
Zumo de piña *pineapple juice*
Zumo de tomate *tomato juice*

Dining in Portugal

Useful Words & Phrases

Reserving a Table

I (we) have a reservation. *Eu (nós) tem(os) uma reserva.*

I'd like a table by a window *Eu queria uma mesa à beira da janela*

I'd like a table outside *Eu queria uma mesa lá fora*

I'd like a quiet table *Eu queria uma mesa tranquila*

Do you have a table for ___ person (people)? *Tem uma mesa para ___ pessoa (pessoas)?*

I would like to reserve a table for ___ person(s) *Eu queria reservar uma mesa para ___ pessoa (pessoas)*

- -1 *uma*
- -2 *duas*
- -3 *três*
- -4 *quatro*

- -5 *cinco*
- -6 *seis*
- -7 *sete*
- -8 *oito*

Tonight *Esta noite*
Tomorrow *Amanhã*
Day after tomorrow *Depois de amanhã*
Sunday *Domingo*
Monday *Segunda*
Tuesday *Terça*
Wednesday *Quarta*
Thursday *Quinta*
Friday *Sexta*
Saturday *Sábado*

Hours of the Day

Portugal operates on a 24-hour clock. Six AM is six o'clock, six PM is 18 o'clock.

1 *um*	13 (1PM) *treze*
2 *dois*	14 (2PM) *catorze*
3 *três*	15 (3PM) *quinze*
4 *quatro*	16 (4PM) *dezasseis*
5 *cinco*	17 (5PM) *dezassete*
6 *seis*	18 (6PM) *dezoito*
7 *sete*	19 (7PM) *dezanove*
8 *oito*	20 (8PM) *vinte*
9 *nove*	21 (9PM) *vinte e um*
10 *dez*	22 (10PM) *vinte e dois*
11 *onze*	23 (11PM) *vinte e três*
12 *doze*	24 (12PM) *vinte e quatro*

Open *Aberto*
Closed *Fechado*
Less *Menos*
More *Mais*
Now *Agora*
Later *Mais tarde*
Before *Antes*
After *Depois*
What time is it? *Que horas são?*

Ordering Meat

Rare *Mal passado*
Medium-rare *Medianamente passado*
Medium *No ponto*
Well done *Bem passado*

Utensils

Knife *Faca*
Fork *Garfo*
Spoon *Colher*
Glass *Copo*
Napkin *Guardanapo*

Special Requests

I am a vegetarian *Eu sou vegetariano*
I am a Vegan *Eu sou Vegan*
I do not eat meat *Eu não como carne*
I am gluten-intolerant. *Eu sou intolerante ao glúten.*
Do you have any dishes that include no wheat, barley or rye? *Tem alguns pratos sem trigo, cevada ou centeio?*
Do you have any dishes suitable for a vegetarian (vegan)? *Tem pratos adequados a vegetarianos (vegans)?*
I do not eat _____. *Eu não como _____.*
I am allergic to _____. *Eu sou alérgico a _____.*
I cannot eat any food containing _____. *Eu não posso comer qualquer comida que tenha _____.*

  -**barley** *cevada*
  -**beef** *carne de vaca*
  -**corn (maize)** *milho*
  -**eggs** *ovos*
  -**fish** *peixe*
  -**gluten** *glúten*
  -**meat** *carne*
  -**milk products** *produtos lácteos*
  -**nuts** *nozes*
  -**peanuts** *amendoins*

P

-raw fish *peixe cru*
-raw meat *carne crua*
-rye *centeio*
-sesame seeds *sementes de sésamo*
-shellfish *marisco*
-soy *soja*
-strawberries *morangos*
-tomatoes *tomate*
-wheat *trigo*

I would like a dish with _____. *Eu queria um prato com _____.*
  -cheese *queijo*
  -eggs *ovos*
  -fish *peixe*
  -seafood *peixe ou marisco*
  -lobster *lagosta*
  -clams *amêijoas*
  -oysters *ostras*
  -mussels *mexilhões*
  -snails *caracóis*
  -lamb *carneiro*
  -beef *carne de vaca*
  -chicken *frango*
  -venison *veado*
  -ham *presunto*
  -pork *carne de porco*
  -sausage *salsicha*
Pitcher of water *Jarro de água*
With ice *Com gelo*

Complaints to the Waiter

This is delicious *Isto é delicioso*

This is too___ *Isto é demasiado___*

  -rare *mal passado*

  -overcooked *bem passado*

  -cold *frio*

  -hot *quente*

I ordered this rare (medium-rare, medium, well-done) *Eu pedi mal passado (medianamente passado, no ponto, bem passado)*

I don't think we ordered this *Eu acho que nós não pedimos isto*

This is not what I ordered *Isto não foi o que eu pedi*

Waiter! *Empregado!*

Waitress! *Empregada!*

This isn't cold *Isto não está frio*

This isn't hot *Isto não está quente*

This isn't fresh *Isto não é fresco*

The Check

May I have the check, please *Podia-me trazer a conta, por favor*

I think there's a mistake on the bill *Acho que há um erro na conta*

Is service included? *O serviço está incluído?*

Do you take credit cards? *Aceita cartões de crédito?*

Where is the toilet? *Onde fica a casa de banho*

Please *Por favor*

Thanks *Obrigado*

Thank you very much *Muito obrigado*

Good evening *Boa noite*

G
U
I
D
E

P

Greetings

Hello *Olá*

Goodbye *Adeus*

Good morning *Bom dia*

Good day *Bom dia*

Good evening *Boa tarde*

Good night *Boa noite*

How are you? *Como estás?*

I'm fine, thank you. *Estou bem, obrigado.*

What is your name? *Qual é o teu nome?*

My name is ____ . *O meu nome é ____.*

Nice to meet you. *Prazer em conhecer-te.*

Yes *Sim*

No *Não*

Please *Por favor*

Thanks *Obrigado*

You're welcome *Bem-vindo*

Excuse me *Desculpe*

I am sorry *Lamento*

Do you speak English? *Falas Inglês?*

I don't understand. *Não percebo.*

Help! *Socorro!*

Ordering Drinks

May we have some tap water (mineral water) *Podíamos beber um pouco de água da torneira (água mineral)*

May I have a glass of red wine, please. *Podia-me trazer um copo de vinho tinto, por favor.*

May I have a glass of white wine, please. *Podia-me trazer um copo de vinho branco, por favor.*

May I have a beer, please. *Podia-me trazer uma cerveja, por favor.*

May I have two beers, please. *Podia-me trazer duas cervejas, por favor.*

A small beer, please *Uma cerveja pequena, por favor*

May I have a bottle of _____, please. *Podia-me trazer uma garrafa de _____, por favor.*

-**whiskey** *whisky*

-**vodka** *vodka*

-**rum** *rum*

-**water** *água*

-**club soda** *refrigerante*

-**tonic water** *água tónica*

-**orange juice** *sumo de laranja*

-**Coca Cola (soda)** *Coca-Cola (refrigerante)*

Portuguese Food

A

Abacate *avocado*

Abacaxi *pineapple*

Abóbor *squash, pumpkin*

Abóbora *hubbard squash, pumpkin*

Abóbora morango *pumpkin*

Abobrinha *zucchini*

Açafrão *saffron*

Açafrão da Índia *turmeric*

Acelga *Swiss chard*

Acepipes variados *assorted hors d'oeuvres*

Açorda *thick, mashed bread soup, often topped with an egg*

Açorda de marisco *bread soup with seafood and coriander*

Açúcar *sugar*

Açúcar granulado *granulated sugar*

Açúcar mascavo *brown sugar*

Açúcar de confeiteiro pulverizado *confectioner's suger*

Adegas *wineries or wine cellars*

Agrião, Agriões *watercress*

Ãgua *water*

   -com gaz *sparkling water*

   -mineral *mineral water*

   -sem gaz *still water*

Aipo *Celery*

Albricoque *apricot*

Alcachôfra *artichoke*

Alcaparras *capers*

Alcarávia *caraway seed*

Alcobaça *a semi-hard ewes' milk cheese*

Alecrim *rosemary*

Alemtejo *a soft ewes' milk cheese*

Alentejana, à *with garlic, paprika and olive oil. In the style of Alentejo.*

Aletria *vermicelli noodles*

Alface *lettuce*

Alfóstigo *pistachio nuts*

A

Alheira *a garlicky Portuguese sausage made with smoked ham and nuts*

Alho *garlic*

Alho frances *leek*

Alho-porro, Alho-porros *leek*

Alimentos *food*

Almôço *lunch*

Almôndêgas *meatballs*

Alperce *apricot*

Alvorca *a grating cheese made from ewes' milk*

Amassada *mashed*

Amêijoas *small, thin-shelled clams*

Ameixa *used for both plums and prunes*

Amêndoas *almonds*

Amendoim *peanut*

Amoras *berries*

Ananás *pineapple*

Anchovas *anchovies*

Anho *lamb*

Arenque *herring*

Arraia *skate, ray (fish)*

Arroz *rice*

Arroz à moda de Valência *kind of paella*

Arroz de marisco *seafood rice*

Arroz de pato *duck with rice*

Arroz de polvo *octopus with rice*

Arroz doce *rice pudding*

Arroz refogado *rice served in an onion and tomato sauce*

As, O *the*

A

P

Assado *roasted*

Assar *bake*

Atum grelhado *grilled tuna fish*

Atum *tuna*

Aveia *oatmeal*

Azeite *olive oil*

Avelâ *hazelnut*

Aves *poultry*

Azêda *sorrel*

Azêdo *sour*

Azeitão *a mild, soft cheese made of ewes' milk*

Azeite *olive oil*

Azeitonas *olives*

B

Bacalhau *dried salt cod*

  -**à Brás** *fried dried cod with fried potatoes and scrambled eggs*

  -**cozido** *salt cod boiled with assorted vegetables*

  -**à gomes de sá** *casserole of salt cod, potato, olives and onion topped with hard boiled eggs*

  -**a portuguêsa** *a casserole of salt cod with potatoes, tomatoes, peppers and onions*

  -**à zé do pipo** *codfish, baked with white sauce olives and purée*

  -**com presunto** *Codfish served with smoked ham*

  -**fresco a portuguesa** *fresh cod steaks fried in oil with eggplant, tomatoes and onions.*

Bacon *bacon*

Bagaceira *Portuguese eau de vie (liquor) made with sugar cane*

Banana *banana*

banha *lard*

Barbo *Barbel (sea fish)*

Batata *potato*

Batata-doce *sweet potato*

Batata gratinada *potatoes au gratin*

Batata inglesa *potatoes*

Batatas fritas *fried potatoes*

Batatas *potatoes*

Batata dôce *sweet potato*

Batido *milk-shake*

Beber *to drink*

Bebida *drink*

Beja *sheep cheese*

Bem cozido *well done meat*

Bem passado *well done meat*

Berbigão, Berbigões *cockles, sometimes refers to mussels*

Berinjela, beringela *eggplant*

Bertalha *vine spinach*

Besugo *sea bream*

Beterraba *beets*

Bica *expresso*

Bife à casa *house steak*

Bife a portuguesa *thin steak topped with a fried egg*

Bife mal passado *rare steak*

Bife *steak, though not necessarily a beefsteak*

Biscoito *cookie*

Bolacha *crackers*

Bolinhos *small meatballs, fishballs etc*

Bõlo *may be ball, cake or pie*
  -de anjo *angel cake*
  -de mel *honey cake*
  -de requeijão *cheese cake*
Borrêgo *lamb*
Branco *white*
Brasa *cooked over charcoal*
Braoas *round sugar cakes*
Bravo *wild*
Brinjela *eggplant*
Broa *cornbread*
Bróculos *brocoli*
Bulo Do Mel *honey cakes*

C

Cabeça *head*
Cabeça de velha *a fine, Portuguese cheese whose odd name means "old lady's head"*
Cabidela *a blood-thickened sauce*
Cabra *goat*
Cabreiro *a strong-favored goat and ewe milk cheese*
Cabrito assado *roast kid*
Cabrito *young goat, kid*
Caça *game*
Cachaça *brazilian sugar cane licquor*
Cacau *cocoa*
Cachorro-quente *hot dog*
Café *coffee*
Café da manhã *breakfast*
Caldeirada de peixe *a bouillabaisse-style fish stew*

Caldeirada *fish stew*

Caldo *broth*

Caldo de carne *bouillon, stock*

Caldo verde *cabbage and potato soup*

Camarão *shrimp*

Camarão graúdo *large prawns, shrimp*

Camarões *shrimps*

Canela *cinnamon*

Cangiquinha *grits*

Canja *chicken broth with meat, mint leaves and lemon juice*

Canja de galinha *chicken soup with chicken livers and pasta (or rice)*

Capão *capon (neutered male chicken)*

caracóis *snails*

Caramelizado *caramelized*

Caranguejo *crab*

Carapau *small mackerel, stickleback-type saltwater fish*

Caril *curry powder*

Carne *meat*
  -de ave *poultry*
  -de boi *beef*
  -de carneiro *lamb*
  -de peito *brisket*
  -de porco *pork*
  -de vaca *beef*
  -de veado *venison*
  -de vitela, o *veal*

Carne assada *roast beef*

C

P

Carne de porco à algarvia *fried pork and clam dish*

Carne picada *chopped meat*

Carneiro *lamb, mutton*

Carnes frias *cold cut (cold sliced meat) platter*

Caseiro *home-made*

Castanha *chestnut*

Castanha do pará *brazil nuts*

Castanha de caju *cashew nuts*

Cataplana *fish/shellfish cooked with ham, onion & pepper*

Cavala *mackerel*

Cebola *onion*

Cebolata, Cebolado *a paste made from fried onions braised until soft, then mashed*

Cebolinha verde *scallions, Spring onions*

Cebolinho *chives*

Cenoura *carrot*

Centeio *rye*

Cereais *cereal*

Cerêjas *cherries*

Cerveja *beer*

Cevada *barley*

Chaputa *black sea bream*

Chá *tea*

Chã *beef round*

Chaleira *kettle*

Chalota *shallot*

Champignons *mushrooms*

Chanfana *a leg of goat or lamb browned in oil and simmered in a covering bath of red wine*

C

P

Chefe de mesa *head waiter, maître d'hôtel*
Cheiro verde *savory (herb)*
Cherne *stone bass*
Chicória *chicory*
Chila *a squash with stringy flesh, like a spaghetti squash*
Choco *cuttlefish*
Chocolate *chocolate*
Chocolate quente *hot chocolate*
Chocos *cuttlefish*
Chouriço *spicy sausage seasoned with paprika and garlic and stored in oil*
Chouriço de sangue *black (blood) pudding*
Churrasco *pork, chicken or other meat cooked on a spit over a wood fire*
Cidra *cider*
C **Clara** *egg white*
Côco *coconut*
Codorniz *quail*
Coelho *domestic, raised rabbit*
Coelho à caçadora *rabbit stew*
Coelho brava *wild rabbit*
Coentro *coriander leaves*
Coentros *coriander seeds*
Cogumelo *mushroom*
Colher *spoon*
Colorau *spicy, red pepper powder*
Colorau-doce *sweet paprika*
Com *with*
Com feijão branco *with white beans*

P

Com gelo *with ice*
Com leite *with milk*
Cominho *cumin*
Compota *jam, stewed fruits*
Confeitado *candied*
Congro *conger eel*
Conserva de fruta *jam*
Conservado *candied*
Conta *the check, bill*
Copo *glass*
Corar *(to) brown*
Corante amarelo *saffron*
Cordeiro *lamb*
Cortar fino *shred*
Corvina *whiting*
Corvino *Corvino, Croaker (sea fish)*
Costeleta *chop, usually boned, cutlet*
  -de borrego *lamb chop*
  -de carneiro *lamb (mutton) chop*
  -de porco *pork chop*
Couscous *couscous*
Couve *cabbage*
Couve de Bruxelas *Brussels sprouts*
Couve-flor *cauliflower*
Couve e feijão *cabbage and beans*
Couve Gallego *Portuguese cabbage*
Couve Lombarda *collard greens or perhaps Kale*
Couvert – manteiga, azeite, azeitonas, queijo, escolha de pães do chefe e amuse bouche *Cover*

C

– butter, olive oil, olives, cheese, bread assortment and an amuse bouche

Cozido *boiled*

Cozido à portuguesa *boiled casserole of meats and beans with rice and vegetables. Served in a broth. Eaten throughout the nation. May include pig's ears, tails and feet.*

Cozinha *kitchen*

Cozinhar *cook*

Cozinhar depressa *cook quickly*

Cozinhar devagar *cook slowly*

Cozinhar em banho maria *cook in double boiler (bain marie)*

Cravo, Cravo da Índia *cloves*

Creme *cream, cream soup*

Creme de Arrôz *rice flour*

Creme de marisco *seafood soup*

Cremoso de lentilhas com foie gras *creamy lentils with foie gras*

Crepe *pancake*

Crepes do céu *pancakes with whipped cream and sweetened fruit*

Crocante *crunchy*

Croissant *croissant*

Croquetes *croquettes*

Croquetes de camarao *shrimp croquettes*

Crú *raw*

D

Damasco *apricot*

Dobrada *tripe (stomach)*

-a modo de porto *chick peas and tripe cooked in water, combined with tomatos, bay leaf, browned onions and garlic and simmered in a casserole*

-com feijao branco *tripe with sausages and white beans*

Doce *candy, sweet*

Doce de amendos *almond flavored dessert*

Doce de chila *the meat of a spaghetti squash boiled with an equal amount of sugar. Used as a sort of jam.*

Doce de leite *a kind of milk pudding*

Doces *desserts*

Dose *serving, portion*

Dourada *bream*

Dourada de mar *sea bream*

E

E

Em *in*

Ementa *menu*

Empada *hot pie, patty*

Empadinha *small tart*

Empadinha de camarão *small shrimp tart*

Encarnada *red*

Enchovas *anchovies*

Endro *dill*

Enguia *eel*

Enguias *eels*

Ensopada,o *a soupy stew, thickened with bread*

-de borrego *lamb stew*

-de coelho *stewed rabbit*

P

-de enguías *eel stew*

-de galinha *chicken stew*

-de lebre *hare stew*

-de perdiz e coelho *partridge and rabbit stew*

Entradas *starters, entrees*

Entrecosto *rib steak*

Entrecosto frito em banha corada *entrecote steak fried in fat*

Ervanço *chickpeas*

Ervas *herbs*

Erva-dôce *fennel, anise*

Ervilhas *peas*

Ervilha partida *dried peas*

Escabeche *marinated*

Escalfado *poached*

Escalfados *poached eggs*

Espargo bravo *wild asparagus*

Espargos *asparagus*

Espetada de tamboril *monkfish kebab*

Espetada *kebab*

Espetada mista *mixed kebab*

Espinafre *spinach*

Estragão *tarragon*

Estrelado *fried*

Estufada *stewed*

Evora *a crumbly ewe and cow milk cheese, quite salty*

Extrato de tomate *ketchup*

E

P

F

Faca *knife*
Faisão *pheasant*
Farinha *flour*
Farinha de avêa *oatmeal*
Farinha de Centeio *rye flour*
Farinha de Milho (Fubá) *cornmeal*
   Creme de Fubá *finest*
   Fubá Médio *medium ground*
   Fubá Grosso *coarse ground*
Farinha de rôsca *breadcrumbs*
Farinha de Trigo *wheat flour*
Farinha Integral *whole wheat flour*
Fatia *slice*
Fatias de alho *sliced garlic*
Fatias frias *cold cut platter*
Fava(s) *broad bean(s)*
Febras *pork steaks*
Febras de porco *a boned fresh ham cooked in red wine with brandy, garlic and cumin*
Feijão *beans*
  -Branco *white beans*
  -de frade *blackeyed peas*
  -de vaca *cow peas*
  -de vagem *green beans, haricot vert*
  -Fava *fava beans*
  -Manteiga *butter beans*
  -Prêto *black beans*
  -Verde *string beans*
Feijoada *dried beans with rice and meat*

Feijoada completa *A stew of black beans, beef (both fresh and salted), tongue, bacon, sausage, pig parts (feet, ears, tails etc) and tomatoes, onions, garlic and seasonings.*

Feijões-verdes *green beans*

Ferver *to boil*

Fiambre *boiled ham*

Figado *liver*

Fígado de vitela grelhado *grilled calf's liver*

Figo *fig*

Figos *figs*

Filé *fillet*

Filetes *fillets*

Filetes de linguado com legumes e gengibre a vapor *Steamed Dover Sole fillet, vegetables with ginger*

filhó *fritter or pancake*

Flan *crème caramel custard*

Flôr de noz moscada *mace (spice)*

Fofas de bacalhau *codfish balls*

Fogão *stove*

Fogo baixo *low heat*

Fôrma *cake pan*

Forno *oven*

Framboesa *raspberry*

Frango *small chicken*

    -com ervilhas *chicken fried and served with peas and onions, with a sauce of pan drippings deglazed with port wine*

    -de carril *roast chicken in hot sauce*

    -guisado *chicken stew with a tomato base*

F

P

-na pucara *chicken casserole*
-no churrasco *barbecued chicken*
Fresca, fresco *chilled*
Frigideira *skillet, frying pan*
Frío *cold*
Fritar *to fry*
Frito *fried*
Fruta *fruit*
Fruta fatiada *sliced fruit*
Frutas doces *plums preserved in a sugary syrup*
Fubá *see Farinha de Milho*
Fumado *smoked*

G

Galatina *aspic*
Galinha *chicken*
Galinha recheada *roasted whole chicken stuffed with a variety of ingredients including sausage, ground meat, eggs, tomatoes, onions and olives*
Galinha salteada *sauteed chicken*
Galinhola *Woodcock (small game bird)*
Gambas *king prawns*
Ganso *goose*
Garfo *fork*
Garrafa *bottle*
Gás *fizzy, carbonated*
Gaspacho *chilled vegetable soup*
Gelado *ice cream*
Gelatina *gelatin*
Geléia *jelly*

G

P

Gema *egg yolk*
Gengibre *ginger*
Gergelim *sesame seed*
Germe de Trigo *wheat germ*
Gila *spaghetti squash*
Glúten *gluten*
Goiaba *guava*
Gondura *lard*
Grao *grain, chickpeas*
Grão de bico *chickpeas*
Gratinada *au gratin*
Grelhado *grilled*
Grelos *sprouts or buds*
Grelhar *grill*
Groselhas *red or black currants*
Groselheira *gooseberry*
Guarnecido *garnished*
Guisado *sautéed then braised in liquid*

H

Hortelã *mint*
Hortelã pimenta *peppermint*

I

Inhame *Yam*
Iscas *casserole*
Iscas a Portugesa *sauteed, marinated calf's liver*
Iscas de figado *marinated liver preparation served with a reduced marinade*
Iogurte *yoghurt*

P

J

Jantar *dinner*
Jardim *garden*
Javali *wild boar*

K

Kaki *persimmon*

L

Lagosta *lobster*
Lagostim *small lobster or prawn*
Lampreia *lamprey*
Lapas *limpets*
Laranja *orange*
   -Bahia *large, seedless, thick-skinned eating orange*
   -Lima *a yellow-green, thin-skinned variety with little flavor; low in acidity*
   -Natal *good eating orange.*
   -Pera *excellent juice orange, thin skin, small-size*
   -Seleta *good all-around orange*
   -Terra *cooking orange*
Lavagante *large lobster, similar to American lobster*
Lebre *hare*
Lebre com feijão branco *hare with white beans*
Legumes *vegetables*
Legumes primaveris *Spring vegetables*
Leitão *baby pork*
Leitão assado *roast suckling pig*
Leite *milk*
Leite condensado *condensed milk*

Leite creme *custard*

Leite de coco *coconut milk*

Lentilha(s) *lentil(s)*

Limão *large lemons or small limes are called this*

Limões *lemons*

Limonada *lemonade*

Linguado *Sole*

Linguado com bananas *baked Sole fillets topped with banana slices*

Linguado grelhado *grilled Sole*

Língua *tongue*

Linguica *spicy pork and red pepper sausage*

Linquisa *a cooked pork sausage tasting of garlic, cinnamon and cumin*

Lombinho *thick slice*

L

Lombinho de porco preto com amêijoas e puré de alcachofras *thick slice of black pork with clams and pureed artichokes*

Lombo *(pork) loin*

Lombo assado com ameixas *roast pork loin with plums*

Lombo com amêijoas *pork loin with clams*

Lombo de robalo grelhado, vinagrete de legumes primaveris *grilled Snook (fish) stuffed with spring vegetables*

Longaniza *large spicy, pork sausage, much like chorizo*

Louro *bay leaf*

Lulas *squid*

P

M

Maçã *apple*

Maçã do pieto *beef brisket*

Maçapão *marzipan*

Macio *tender, soft*

Macarrão *macaroni*

Madeirense, à *Madeira style, with garlic, onions and tomatoes*

Magret de pato com morangos, Porto *Duck breast with strawberries, Port*

Maisena *corn starch*

Mal passado *underdone*

Malasado *deep fried pastry dredged in sugar*

Malassadas *sweet doughnuts*

Mamão *papaya*

Maneira de, à *in the style of*

Manga *mango*

   -Familia *Oval shaped, large, meaty mango. Green skinned, almost no fibers.*

   -Rosa *large and round in shape, not very fibrous, colorful orange rose skin and meat*

   -Espada *medium-sized mango with green skin and oval shape, yellow-green meat*

Manjericão *basil*

Manjerona *marjoram*

Manteiga *butter*

Manteiga de amendoim *peanut butter*

Marisco *seafood*

Marmelo *quince*

Massa *pasta*

Massa de pimentão *paste of chilli peppers*

Massa folhada *puff pastry*

Medalhões de vitela *veal medallions*

Médio *medium cooked (as in meats, steaks)*

Mel *honey*

Melaço *molasses*

Melado *molasses*

Melãncia *watermelon*

Melão *melon, sometimes describes a dinner roll*

Merendeiras *small, fresh sheep milk cheese stored in oil*

Mercado *market*

Merenda *light snack*

Mesa *table*

Mesclun de salada *mesclun salad*

Mexido *scrambled*

Mexilhão, Mexilhões *mussel, mussels*

Migas *small cubes of pork and beef coated in red pepper paste and fried*

Mil folhas *puff pastry*

Milho *corn*

Milho Verde *Corn on the cob*

Minhota, à *Minho style, cooked in vinho verde with chopped ham*

Miolos *brains*

Miúdos *giblets*

Moda..., à *in the style of...*

Moleas (de vitela) *(veal) sweetbreads*

Molho *several, a bunch*

Môlho *sauce*

M

P

-branco *white sauce, bechamel*
-de maças *apple sauce*
-de Soja *soy sauce*
-de tomate *ketchup*
-inglês *Worcestershire Sauce*
Morangos *strawberries*
Morcela *blood sausage*
Mostarda *mustard*
Mousse de chocolate *chocolate mousse*
Muito mal passado *very rare steak*

N

Nabo *turnip*
Nêsperas *loquat (fruit)*
No forno *oven-baked*
Noz *walnut*
Noz moscada *nutmeg*

N

O

O nosso Bacalhau *our codfish*
Omelete *omelette*
Oregano *oregano*
Orelhas *ears*
Ostra(s) *oyster(s)*
Ovo *egg*
Ovos *eggs*
-duros *hardboiled eggs*
-escalados *poached eggs*
-estrelados *fried eggs*
-mexidos *scrambled eggs*

P

-**moles** *sauce of egg yolk and sugar*
-**quentes** *softboiled eggs*

P

Padeira, à *baked in a hot oven*
Pãezinhos de pó Royal *baking powder bisquits*
Paio *garlicky, smoked pork sausage*
Palmito *heart of palm*
Panqueca *pancake*
Pão *bread*
Pão integral *wholemeal bread*
Papo(s) de anjo *butter cake(s) with syrup*
Papo seco *bread or roll without butter*
Paprika *paprika*
Pargo *red snapper*
Parmesão *parmasan cheese*
Passa *raisin*
Passa de Corinto *currant*
Pasta de amêndoas *almond paste, marzipan*
Pasta manteiga de amendoim *peanut butter*
Pastéis *patty-shaped food, may either be savory or sweet*
Pastéis de bacalhau *salt cod in a crust*
Pastéis de nata *custard tart*
Pastél *tart, pastry*
Pastelería *pastries*
Pastélinho *small tart or pie*
Paté *pate*
Patinho *duckling*
Pato (bravo) *(wild) duck*

P

Peito de frango *chicken breast*

Peixe *fish*

Peixe espada *swordfish*

Peixelua *basking shark*

Pepino *cucumber*

Pequeno almoço *breakfast*

Pêra *pear*

Perdiz *partridge (game bird)*

Peri Peri *a hot and sour sauce made of hot chili peppers, garlic, onions, horseradish, tomatoes, and lemon juice*

Perna de carne *leg (of meat)*

Peru *turkey*

Pescada *fish similar to hake or whiting*

Pescado *any kind of food fish*

Pêssego *peach*

Picado *hash*

Pimenta *pepper*

Pimenta da caiena *cayenne pepper*

Pimenta da Jamaica *allspice*

Pimenta do *pepper*

Pimenta malagueta *chili*

Pimentão *green pepper*

Pimentão-doce *sweet pepper*

Pimento do reino *black pepper*

Pimienta *pepper (plant)*

Piri piri *hot chili sauce, see Peri Peri*

Pistáchios *pistachios*

Pizza *pizza*

Polvo *octopus*

P

Polvo assado com batata-doce *Grilled octopus with sweet potato*

Pombo *squab, pigeon, dove*

Pombo cozido com arroz *dove cooked with rice*

Porco *pork*

Porco a alentejana *pork with clams*

Porto *port*

Posta de carne *a slice of beef*

Prato do dia *dish of the day*

Pratos de carne *meat dishes*

preço fixo, a *prix fixe meal, all included price*

Presunto *cured ham*

Presunto de lamego *ham from pigs fed acorns from cork oaks*

Primeiro Prato *appetizer, first course*

Pudim *pudding*

-**de nozes** *custard with cinnamon and walnuts*

-**de ovos** *custard flavoured with lemon and cinnamon*

-**Flan** *crème caramel, custard*

-**Portugues** *Orange custard*

Purê *mashed, puréed*

Q

Queijadas de sintra *unsweetened patties made of cheese, eggs and almonds*

Queijo *cheese*

-**arreganhado** *a mild and mellow cheese made from the first milk drawn from the ewe which doesn't contain much fat*

-da IIha *a hard cows' milk cheese from the Azores resembling a mature Cheddar, used mainly for cooking. Also ca lled queijo da Terra*

-da Serra *a famous high-fat sheep cheese. Similar to Brie, it is eaten runny or when firm and pungent.*

-do ceu *a cheese-based dessert*

-Petit Suisse *cream cheese*

Queijos frescos *fresh cheese*

Queijos nacionais e estrangeiros *cheeses local and imported*

Quente *warm*

Quiabo *okra*

Quinta *country estate/villa*

R

Rã *Frogs in a creamy dill sauce*

Rabaçal *a soft, mild curd cheese with goat and sheep milk*

Rabanadas *a sweetened, fried bread dessert*

Rabanete *radish*

Rabo *tails (oxtail)*

Raia *skate*

Raia blanca *white skate*

Rainha Claudia *a type of plum*

Raiz forte *horseradish*

Ramo de cheiras *a Portuguese bouquet garni (herb bag or sachet)*

Rapadura *brown sugar*

Recheado, recheio *stuffed or stuffing*

Refogado *onion and tomato sauce*

R

P

Regar *baste*

Repôlho *Cabbage*

Repôlho vermelho *red cabbage*

Requeijão *Ricotta-like cheese*

Risoto de mexilhão e camarão *Seafood risotto with mussels and shrimp*

Risoto *risotto*

Risoto de açafrão e leite de coco com camarão *risotto with safron and coconut milk and prawns*

Rissois de camarao *Shrimp pies*

Robalo *snook, sea bass*

Rodovalho *halibut*

S

Sabula de Vinha *pickled onions*

Sal *salt*

Salada *salad*

Salgado *salted*

Salmão *salmon*

Salmão marinado *marinated salmon*

Salmonete *red mullet*

Saloio *Cow's milk cheese eaten when fresh*

Salpicão *a fine-grained, smoked pork sausage*

Salsa *parsley*

Salsa *gravy or sauce*

Salsicha(s) *sausage(s)*

Salteado *sautéed*

Salva *sage*

Sanduiche *sandwich*

Sangue *blood*

Sangue, em *rare, as meat*

Santola recheada *stuffed crab*

Sapateira *crab*

Sarapatel *a stew made with pig offal including: heart, liver, tongue, stomach and blood*

Sarda *mackerel*

Sardinhas *sardines*

Sardinhas na brasa *grilled sardines*

Sargo *silver bream*

Saude *cheers!*

Saval, Savelha *shad (anadromous fish)*

Séco *dry or dried*

Segundo Prato *main course*

Segurelha *basil*

Sementes de áipo *celery seed*

Sementes de papoula *poppy seed*

Semolina *cream of wheat*

Senhora *woman*

Senhor *man*

Serviço incluido *service is included*

Sobremesa *dessert*

Sojita *soy flour*

Sôlha *plaice (flounder-like fish)*

Sopa *soup*

  -de batata e agriao *potato and watercress soup*

  -de camarao e mexilhao *mussel and shrimp soup*

  -de coentros *soup of coriander, bread and a poached egg*

S

-de feijao *bean soup*

-de feijao verde *green bean soup*

-de grao *chickpea soup*

-de legumes *vegetable soup*

-de legumes do dia *Daily made vegetable soup*

-de marisco *shellfish soup*

-de peixe *fish soup*

-do dia *soup of the day*

-do Mar *Shellfish soup*

-seca *shredded meat layered in a pot with boiled potatoes and carrots, bread and mint, covered with broth and oven cooked until dry*

Sorvete *ice cream*

Suco, Sumo *juice*

-de ananás *pineapple juice*

-de laranja *orange juice*

-de maçã *apple juice*

-de tomate *tomato juice*

Supermercado *supermarket*

Supremo de pintada *Guinea Fowl Breast*

T

Tâmara *date*

Tangerina *Tangerine*

Tártaro de salmão *salmon tartar*

Tarte de cacau quente com morangos temperados *Hot cocoa pie with tangerine ice cream*

Tasca *tavern*

Temperado *spicy*

Tiramisu de peras bêbedas em vinho do Porto *pear tiramisu in Porto wine (port)*

Timo or Tomilho *thyme*

Tomate *tomato*

Toranja *grapefruit*

Tordos com arroz *birds with rice*

Torrada(s) *toast*

Torta *cake roll*

Torta de cenoura *carrot cake*

Tortilha (de mariscos) *omelette (with chopped shellfish)*

Toucinho *bacon, lard*

Toucinho defumado *smoked bacon*

Transmontana, a *in the Trasos-Montes style, with beans, sausage and onions*

Tripas à moda do Porto *tripe dish with veal beans and spicy sausage*

Tripa *tripe*

Trufas *truffles*

Truta *trout*

Tufas (grelhadas) *squid (grilled)*

U

Uva *grape*

Uvas *grapes*

V

Vaca *beef from aged cows*

Vaca cozida *boiled beef*

Vaca guisada *beef stew*

Vagem *green beans, haricot vert*

Vapor, à *steamed*

Vegetais *vegetables*

Vegetariano *vegetarian*

Vieiras salteadas com cenoura confitada com citrinos *Sautéed scallop shell with carrot and kumquats*

Vinagre *vinegar*

Vinagrete *vinaigrette*

Vinha D' Alhos *fish or pork in vinegar and garlic*

Vinho branco *white wine*

Vinho da casa *house wine*

Vinho de porto *port wine*

Vinho doce *sweet wine*

Vinho seco *dry wine*

Vinho tinto *red wine*

Vinho verde *semi-sparkling, young wine*

Vitela *veal*

Vitela curada em flor de sal *veal cured in sea salt*

Viveiro de mariscos *shellfish stew*

X

Xarope *syrup*